$lash or Splash?

control your cash

332

liam croke

NEW HOLLAND

Published in 2009 by New Holland Publishers (UK) Ltd
London • Cape Town • Sydney • Auckland
www.newhollandpublishers.com
Garfield House, 86–88 Edgware Road, London W2 2EA, United Kingdom
80 McKenzie Street, Cape Town 8001, South Africa
Unit 1, 66 Gibbes Street, Chatswood, NSW 2067, Australia
218 Lake Road, Northcote, Auckland, New Zealand

10 9 8 7 6 5 4 3 2 1

A catalogue record for this book is available from the British Library

ISBN 978 1 84773 571 3

Publishing Director: Rosemary Wilkinson
Publisher: Aruna Vasudevan
Project Editor:Julia Shone
Editor: Sally MacEachern
Design and Cover design: District-6
Production: Melanie Dowland

Reproduction by Pica Digital (Pte) Ltd, Singapore
Printed and bound in India by Replika Press

The paper used to produce this book is sourced from sustainable forests.

contents

introduction

why?

I am sure you are asking 'why'?

- **Why do I need a book about finance?**
- **What does it have to do with me?**
- **Why should I read it?**

Well, the reality is money really does make the world go round. Without it, how can you achieve your dreams? Buy that scooter or car? Go to Ibiza? Buy your iPhone? Go to college? Make more money?

This book aims to give you the skills to do all this. But first, a few brutal facts. This is what is happening now in our country on an average day:

£ every 10 minutes a property will be repossessed

£ a person every 4.5 minutes will be declared bankrupt

£ 2,915 people will be made redundant

£ the government will repay £91 million in interest just to service our national debt

£ the average household debt will increase by £1.90

£ the average house will decrease in value by £95

£ consumers will save on average £2.84

£ £578 million will be withdrawn from cash machines

£ the citizens advice bureau will deal with over 7,000 new debt problems

£ the average car will cost £16.80 to run

- £ 902,000 homeowners have missed a mortgage repayment in the past six months

- £ research shows that 50 percent of 18 to 34 year olds had debts up to £10,000 and 20 percent had debts greater than £10,000

- £ nearly a third of young people has no savings at all

- £ research shows that over 5 million people in the uk are seriously struggling to make ends meet - this equates to 1 in 10 people, or 11 percent of our population

- £ 10.3 million people in the uk are now relying on credit cards and other methods of borrowing to pay for their everyday living expenses

- £ research shows that 1 in 3 students are constantly overdrawn

- £ 2 in 5 students admit to being completely disorganized about their money

- £ 1 in 6 uk consumers feel they are unable to cover their current credit commitments

- £ students who started at university last year can expect to graduate owing over £17,500

- £ the average weekly allowance given to children from parents is £6.13

I'm sure you're now asking: '*why does any of this concern me?*'

Well, most people are terrible at managing their money. In general, we are not taught about it at school. Our parents never really speak about it, so most of us do not understand how money or finance works.

The purpose of this book is, therefore, simple:
- it is to make sure that you will understand how money works
- it will help equip you with the skills to manage your money properly, skills which will hopefully last you a lifetime

- and, more importantly, prevent you from becoming one of the frightening statistics, which I have just listed.

Becoming better at saving and spending money does not require in-depth knowledge of financial products such as credit cards, mortgages, and so on; it is about understanding underlying principles and developing skills – and that is what this book aims to give you. How you choose to apply it is up to you – and possibly your parents, as well.

We live in a money-driven culture. But while money is an important feature of your life, being able to put it into perspective will help you develop a healthy attitude towards it.

> *'Teenagers should begin learning basic financial skills as early as possible … it can help prevent students from making poor decisions later … that can take years to overcome.'*
> – Alan Greenspan, ex-chairman of the US Federal Reserve, September 2003

As adults we make decisions that we believe and think are right but which sometimes are really ill-informed. How many times have you heard people say, *'With hindsight I would have done something different?'* Well, with foresight and knowledge you hopefully will not make as many mistakes about money as your parents, or their parents before them, have done – and that starts right here, right now with this book.

This book outlines the economy and the role that the government plays in keeping it on track. The 'credit crunch' and recession are explained briefly, as are credit cards and mortgages, which might both seem a way off now, but relate to your life and also understanding your parents' and your family's finances. I also deal with how to manage your money and show you how to develop your entrepreneurial skills. You will also see that when it comes to investing your own money, you have several different options open to you.

Saving money, spending it wisely, sharing and earning money and planning for the future are important skills – all of which you will need as you grow older. *Stash or Splash?* should give you the base from which to do this.

It is often said that money is neither good nor bad but that it's what's done with it that counts. In my opinion, never a truer word was spoken!

– liam croke, 2009

chapter 1
making money

The majority of your money at the moment probably comes from a weekly allowance given to you by your Mum or Dad, but I'm sure *'money doesn't grow on trees'* is an expression they frequently use so you would, I am sure, like to be less dependent on them.

But if you want more money in your pockets, in most instances, you are going to have to earn it. That's where having a part-time job comes in.

But why work? What are the benefits?

£ **extra money in your pocket to do what you want**

£ **you're not dependent on your parents**

£ **it may give you the chance to learn new things**

£ **it may give you the chance to meet new people and make new friends**

£ **it may empower you by giving the opportunity to develop new skills that could last you a lifetime**

The most common ways of earning money are from:

• **starting your own business**

• **working for someone else**

We'll start off by looking at working for yourself and look at some ideas beyond the usual paper rounds, busking or babysitting.

OK, so here goes with some alternative suggestions to the norm:

£ **a car cleaning business**

£ **a house-painting service**

£ **a messenger or delivery service**

There are, of course, many, many other ideas that you can probably come up with yourself. So, get a sheet of paper and write down anything that you think people might be willing to pay you for doing (that's legal, of course...).

job hunting

Apart from working for yourself, the other way to earn money is to work for someone else. But, believe me, searching for a job can be hard work in itself, even in a healthy job market. So, how do you start?

Narrow down exactly what you want to do, in terms of:

☑ **the type of job you want**

☑ **the location**

☑ **the hours**

and, finally,

☑ **the pay**

You might not be able to find a job that ticks all of these boxes but if you want – or need – to earn extra money, and taking into account the current employment situation, you should try to find one that ticks as many boxes as possible.

Finding a job in the past few years may have been quite an easy thing to do but unfortunately now, with the 'credit crunch', finding a job – even a summer job – takes planning, effort and determination.

So, while you are looking for a job in the classified ads in papers, online, through blog sites, among other things, you can also help yourself by:

* **getting to know your parent's friends a bit better**
Always avoided them? Get to know them a little bit better; they may have interesting jobs and may be able to help you find a job.

* **dress appropriately**
You can still be yourself: dress in your usual style but just be aware of how appropriate it is for whatever you're doing, whether it be going for an interview or working in an office – don't look as if you're nipping out for a coffee or hanging out with your mates, if it's inappropriate.

* **beware of the competition**
Competition for jobs is fierce, especially now, so in reality not only will you be up against people of your own age but older, more experienced people as well, who might be more hungry for the job as they need to pay bills. Think about what makes you the more attractive option?

* **better luck outdoors?**
Think outside the box. In the summer, for example, there might be more jobs available in water parks, summer camps, music festivals, and so on, dealing with comparatively younger audiences, where your skills might be a real asset.

* **surf the net for jobs**
Love the net? Then use it! Check out websites advertizing part-time jobs in your area, but don't make it your sole method of job hunting.

* **hit the streets**
Go into local offices and stores and ask if they have any vacancies? They might not be openly advertising at present but that doesn't mean that they won't need to in the future.

* **keep smiling**
No matter how bad it gets, try to keep smiling. Studies show that employers look for these things in people of all ages – enthusiasm, positive attitude and hard work are key attributes.

what employers look for in teenagers

They want motivated people, who:

- arrive to work on time

- have a positive attitude

- work hard

- are are respectful of others and themselves

- show leadership qualities

- do the best job they can do

Remember you need to show your employer that they were right to take you on, both for the job they are asking you to do now, as well as for future job positions.

it's the attitude

Attitude is important. If you adopt the *'I hate this job'* attitude then you will get nothing out of it. If, on the other hand, you look at this job as an opportunity to learn how a business operates from the inside out then you will get a whole lot out of it.

Think of Gordon Ramsay, for example. He learned how to become a great chef and restaurateur by first working in a restaurant. He gathered knowledge, information and skill at an early age and used this to become a multimillionaire and one of the most recognizable names and faces in international cuisine today.

applying for a job

OK, we know it's not going to be easy getting a job.

There will be a lot of competition, so you have to have the confidence and belief that you are the best person for that role – if you don't believe it, how will your employer?

You might have to complete an application form where you fill out some basic information like:

 your name and address

 date of birth

 contact numbers/email

 previous work experience

 references – from a reliable source (teachers/past employers) – but make sure it's someone who will give you a good character reference – and don't forget to ask them for permission first! That's essential.

 parental consent – some employers may want consent in writing from your parents before they even interview you for a job

pretty please...

If you get an interview, be polite during and after you leave.

Drop a little 'one-liner' (note or email) to your interviewer thanking them for taking the time to meet with you. You never know, it might soon be you who is being congratulated by that person for getting the job. It also pays to be polite as it is a very small world.

Use everything at your disposal that might give you the edge over your competition. Small things that you may feel are unimportant can, and often do, in fact, make all the difference.

It also doesn't cost you anything to:

☑ **dress smartly**

☑ **arrive on time**

☑ **be polite**

… It doesn't cost you anything, *but* you can potentially gain a lot.

Let me tell you quickly about my nephew, Brian, who is 18. During the summer last year he got himself a job with a bread delivery company. Now he is not the happiest person in the morning but for eight weeks of the summer he was up at 6 a.m. every morning delivering bread to shops and stores locally. He didn't give up, he knew what he had to do and got on with it. He was respectful of the older people he was working with and they were very happy with him. Now, when he applies for other jobs he is guaranteed at least one glowing reference from a previous employer. And that's really important.

You can find that perfect job – if you are willing to work hard and be persistent. Take each job with the attitude that you will do your very best to make it work and gain something from it.

The harder you work and the more responsible you are – the greater the chance you have of finding and keeping that perfect job.

spending your cash!

We all like to spend money – of course we do, it's a natural instinct. The reality is that we are not all millionaires and can't just buy anything and everything that we want.

Most of us are given, or earn, a certain amount of money each week and have to watch what we spend it on. If we think a bit more about our spending and plan in advance what we are going to buy, purchase or invest in, we can actually get more for our money.

A '*smart spender*' isn't someone who is mean or a 'Scrooge'; he or she is someone who is really good with money and thinks first before he or she parts with any money.

It is important to have enough income to pay for such things as your phone credit or your sports/club membership, for example, so set aside what that costs so that you can cover these '*must-pay*' expenses first.

You can then choose to spend any money that you have left over on whatever you want (within reason, of course!).

is it a 'need' or a 'want'?

Before you start spending your money – and before we discuss making a budget – it is important to know the difference between a '*need*' and a '*want*'.

- *needs* are the things that you must have in order to live, e.g. food, water, clothing and shelter

- *wants* are things that are non-essentials – you might want a new DVD, a new outfit or a new TV, but you can survive without them

Most people have more *wants* than *needs*, as you can imagine.

The problem comes when people find it difficult to tell the difference between the two. And, there is a crucial difference.

So, what's the answer?

Two tips:

£ you should spend your money on your *needs* first

£ when your *needs* are cared for then you start talking about your *wants*

budget it!

A budget is basically a map of where your money comes from and where it goes. It shows you exactly what you are spending your money on and highlights any areas that you could potentially cut back on.

How do you create a budget?

It really is quite simple. Using a scrap of paper and a pen, draw a line down the middle of the page and write '*income*' on the left-hand side and '*outgoings*' on the right (*see below*).

Under '*income*' write down all the ways you receive money and under '*outgoings*' the things you spend your money on. Your budget for one month might look like this:

income (£)		outgoings (£)	
Job	50	Books/Magazines	10
Savings	5	CDs	10
Parents	25	Food	15
		Phone credit	20
total	**£80**	**total**	**£55**

If your income is greater than your outgoings (*as in the example above*), that's great – you have a surplus each month and can do what you please with it, spend, save or invest it.

If, on the other hand, your expenses are greater than your income then you have a problem, or, in business terms, a '*deficit*'.

The answer to this deficit is simple. You have to:

£ **spend less,** or

£ **earn more**

Spending less: a budget is a great way to discover what you are spending too much money on. Maybe your phone credit, clothes or food are too expensive? Knowing exactly how much you are spending and on what items will help you manage your money better.

You will be able to know, for example, that this month you are going to have to give that Chelsea match a miss, or put off going to Glastonbury until next year because you just don't have enough money. But, what you can also do is build up a surplus over the months to compensate for these purchases by saving £5 or so each month (or whatever you can afford) and then use this sum to splurge on those wants.

After a while you will become used to managing your money on a monthly basis. It is always worth keeping a written record of your incomings and outgoings, whether it be handwritten, on your phone or on your laptop or computer – no matter how tedious it may seem at the time.

why budget?

I know a lot of you might think that creating a budget is a hassle and a bit of a waste of time but, on the other hand, by not making one you could lose sleep worrying about whether you have enough money.

Recent surveys have found that 80 percent of 18–24 year olds don't budget. However, keeping within your monetary limits is vital if you want to take control of your finances and not let them control you! Some good reasons to make a budget are that it gives you:

£ **a very good picture of your present financial situation**

£ **information to show others that you can manage your money (your bank manager will like this)**

£ **data to identify any areas in which you are overspending each month**

£ **information to prevent you from running up debts that could take years to repay in full (e.g. credit cards, student loans, unrealistically high-interest loans)**

10 ways to reduce your spending

1. practise self-control
Don't make an impulse purchase. Give yourself some time before you finally make up your mind.

2. set a spending limit
Before you go shopping set a limit on how much you can spend.

3. make a shopping list before you leave home

4. research your product before you purchase it
This will ensure you are getting the best value for money, especially with expensive purchases, such as an iMac. Research the quality and the reputation of the product. Check other stores, high-street and online, and compare prices. Do '*comparison shopping*': it can lead to huge savings and better-quality purchases for you in the end.

5. keep a track of your spending
As I said earlier, this makes you stick to your spending limits.

6. consider used instead of new items
Don't forget about the library if you want to read a particular book or listen to a DVD or CD. Look for used games or DVDs at second-hand stores. Check out clothes at charity shops. And, of course, there's always ebay...

7. take good care of what you buy -
It can be expensive to replace things, so look after them.

8. do not buy something just because someone you know has it!

9. if you do not have the cash then do not buy it!

10. do not borrow money from your friends and family-
   You might find it hard to repay them and this could lead to bad feelings. Is it worth losing a close friend over money?

Sharing your time and money

You might think that the only reason to save and spend money is to take care of yourself. In a way you are right, but if you use some of your money and your spare time to help those who are less fortunate than you, it will really feel good to know that you are putting something back in and making a difference to someone. And, it makes you appreciate what you have, which we all take a bit for granted at times.

Here are just a few ideas that will help you get more involved in sharing your time and money with others:

- **donate a regular percentage of what you earn each month to the charity you feel is most deserving.**

- **join or start an organization in your local area that helps others.**

- **take part in, or organize, a walk or run that raises money for a local charity.**

chapter 2
banking

Modern-day banking can be traced back to the Italian cities of Venice, Florence and Genoa, where merchants gave loans to princes to fund their lavish lifestyles and to finance their wars. The Bardi and Peruzzi families dominated 14th-century banking, particularly in Florence, and soon they became so successful that they started opening branches throughout Europe. But both of these families lost huge sums of money to Edward III (King of England 1327–77). He wanted money to finance the Hundred Years' War (1337–1453) against France. But Edward never paid them back and they went bust. *Sound familiar?*

The most famous medieval Italian bank was that of the Medicis, set up by Giovanni Medici in 1397. Like the Bardis and Peruzzis, the Medicis extended loans to merchants and royalty but they also enjoyed the distinction of being the main banker to the Pope. Business from His Holiness generated higher profits for the bank than any of its other activities and, because of this, more banks were quickly set up.

During the 17th and 18th centuries, it was the British who improved upon Italian-banking techniques and this was all down to London goldsmiths. By the middle of the 17th century the goldsmiths' traditional business of making objects from gold and silver had ceased because of the Civil War (1642–6). Forced into an alternative way of making a living, they began accepting deposits of precious metals for safekeeping. In return the goldsmiths would issue a receipt for the deposit. These receipts were circulated as a form of money. The goldsmiths came to realize that not all of their depositors would demand their gold or silver back at the same time, so they cleverly started issuing more receipts (money) than the metal in their vaults.

I'm sure you're asking why is this relevant to you? Well, what can you do with your hard-earned cash other than put it in a bank? Keep it at home, in a drawer, where it won't earn any extra money for you? But then you run the risk of losing it all in the blink of an eye if your house catches fire or if it is stolen. What sense is there in that? The answer is a bit of a no-brainer.

However, opening a bank account is actually quite a big step to take because you are putting your money in someone else's hands. You are trusting a bank to look after your money responsibly and, so, before you do this, it is essential to understand how banks operate, particularly in the current credit crunch.

what is a bank?

Put simply a bank sells financial services. These come in the form of house mortgages, car loans, personal loans, student loans, credit cards, savings accounts, retirement accounts and so on.

You will go to the bank essentially for two reasons:

1. to deposit your money in a safe place

2. because you want to borrow money to buy a car/pay for college/ expand a business, or do other things that require money you do not have

But where do banks get the money that they lend?

£ from people who open bank accounts with them – if people didn't put money into banks then they would have little or no money to lend

£ from each other – banks lend vast sums of money from and to each other each year

So, your savings and borrowed money essentially help form a big pool of money that banks then use to make loans. All of this money, by the way, does not belong to the bank's shareholders or its board of directors, it belongs to you and other deposit holders. This is why bankers have an obligation not to take unreasonable risks when they give out loans. It seems that this obligation has been forgotten in recent times, however, as banks have often made reckless loans to people who clearly can't afford them in the first place and also to property developers who thought the bottom would never drop out of the property market. (I will deal with this issue in more depth later in the book.)

Because banks are a business they want to make money and they do this in a variety of ways.

If a bank gives you money, there is absolutely no guarantee that they will ever get their money back. So, why do they take the risk? Well, the answer is twofold:

- **the opportunity to make more money** –
  For example, suppose a bank lends me £20,000. In order to make a profit the bank charges 'interest' on this loan – interest is the price borrowers pay for using someone else's money. If they charge me 10 percent, then I will repay them a total of £22,000, so they get back their initial £20,000 and make £2,000 profit.

- **they can reduce their risk by getting security or collateral** –
  This could come in the form of a house or a car. If I do not repay my home loan, they can repossess the property and try to recoup what they are owed in full.

An unsecured loan, on the other hand, would be for something like a holiday. If you fail to repay that loan, they can't repossess your two weeks in Ibiza. So, because this is a riskier loan they may charge you a higher rate of interest.

For example, the following shows comparative rates of interest:

- **Secured loan (house loan):** 4.5 percent on the capital sum

- **Unsecured loan (holiday loan):** 10 percent on the capital sum

in the real world

... In the real world, before a bank will lend money to you – whether it be secured or unsecured – they will first take the following into consideration:

- your ability to repay the loan

- whether you have a good history of repaying loans

- how much and what type of other loans or credit you currently have

how do i choose a bank?

In the United States in the 1950s you were given a new toaster if you opened an account with a certain bank, so if you needed a new toaster you simply opened your account with that bank!

Nearly 60 years later, things haven't changed that much. Banks are still offering gimmicks or incentives to attract new customers. These can come in the form of cash offers, vouchers, wallcharts, video games, film vouchers, and so on. However, you should in no way be swayed or influenced by gifts or offers of cash when choosing a bank. A freebie doesn't mean the bank in question is right for you or even offers you the services you may want or need to survive financially.

First and foremost, you should start by shopping around to find out which banks offer the best services, the highest interest rates and the lowest fees. Most banks offer student rates – with special interest rates, overdraft limits, loans and so on. A few banks don't charge any fees at all, but some do if your account falls below a certain level, while other banks charge fees for particular transactions like withdrawing money from an ATM machine. All these fees add up.

So, what should be on your checklist when choosing a bank?

How about the following five points for starters?

☑ **what rate of interest does it pay for the money in your current/savings account?**

☑ **what rate of interest does it charge if you want a student loan? It better be 0 percent.**

☑ **is the bank in a convenient location and are its business hours convenient for you? Do they offer an online banking service?**

☑ **is your money safe and protected under the deposit protection scheme?**

☑ **do they provide a courteous and efficient service?**

Before you open an account with anyone ask your friends or family if they are happy with their banks and also if they would recommend them. Don't forget to do some '*comparison shopping*' because all banks are not the same! Personal recommendations are important – but remember, if you're asking someone older, their criteria might be different to your own.

Which services do banks provide?

Banks usually offer the following to their customers:

- **mortgages**

- **savings accounts**

- **current accounts**

- **credit cards**

- **car loans**

- **student loans**

- **foreign exchange**

- **debit/cash cards**

- **online banking**

- **bill payment service – you can set up a direct debit each month from your account to pay bills**

- **business banking – this refers to a section in a bank that deals with loans for start-up and existing businesses**

- **stockbroking facility – you can buy and sell shares through a bank**

- **international payments – transfer of money to or from a bank in another country**

- **home insurance**

- **life assurance**

- **car/travel and pet insurance**

- **pension saving accounts**

how do i open an account?

OK, once you have decided who you are going to open your account with, what next?

When you enter the bank of your choice, you'll have to complete an application form. Don't forget to take some form of photo ID with you and something that verifies where you live, as you will be asked for both when opening your account.

If you are under 16 then you may need a parent or guardian with you who can confirm who you are and where you live. They may even be asked to cosign the application until you turn 18.

the magic of compound interest

Once you have an account, how the interest is calculated can greatly affect your savings. So, let's assume your bank pays interest on their savings account every month. As each month goes by you will earn interest on everything in your account. The great thing about this is that you will earn interest on previous interest payments. This is compound interest. Remember your initial deposit will also earn interest each month and continues to earn interest over and over again.

Let me show you what I mean. If you lodged £1,500 into an account and did not touch it for 5 years and your rate of interest was 3 percent paid every month, as you can see from the following table, the interest you are earning is going up.

year	balance	interest earned
1	£1500.00	£45.68
2	£1545.68	£47.07
3	£1592.75	£48.33
4	£1641.08	£49.91
5	£1690.99	£51.44

Therefore, this is another question you should ask when opening up an account – how often is the interest earned applied to your account? The more frequent the better!

What happens to your money once it is lodged into your account?

Bankers claim that once you and other account holders lodge your money with their bank, they 'put most of it to work.'

Let me explain how this works.

Most of your money is held in reserve but the remainder is loaned out to people who need to borrow money in order to buy a house, car, business equipment, and so on.

Remember a bank is not there just to provide a service to us, it is in business to make money. And here's how:

 it pays 3 percent interest to people with money on deposit – savers. So if you have £1,000 on deposit you will earn £30 in one year.

 it charges 10 percent to people who want to borrow money to go on holiday, for example – borrowers. So if you borrow £1,000, you will have to pay £100 in interest over one year.

The difference between what a financial institution charges for loans and what it gives to savers, that bank keeps.

how do banks set the rate of interest?

This is a great question and will depend on two things:

- **how many people want to borrow money**

- **how much money they have available to lend**

If banks have plenty of money to lend but people don't want to borrow, then interest rates will be low in order to attract borrowers. The reverse happens when money supply is short and demand for money is high, then interest rates go up.

As a potential borrower in the future you want interest rates to be as low as possible.

Is the rate ever 0 percent? Well, this has happened in the UK in 2009. Some mortgage holders who borrowed, for example, £360,000 have monthly repayments of 1 pence per month.

How? Well the Bank of England (BOE) wants us to spend money, so it lowered interest rates to .5 percent and some lenders were offering rates of .5 percent below the Bank of England lending rate. At the time they set the rate, the BOE rate might have been 4 percent, and little did the lenders know then that rates would come down so low.

why do banks fail?

The answer to this question is quite simple – banks fail when they are in danger of running out of cash to meet their financial obligations.

If you hold money on deposit with a bank and you fear that it is about to go bankrupt, what would you do? Withdraw your money of course! People fear that if a bank fails then they will lose all of their money, so they panic and withdraw their savings. *See box on page 31.*

This happened in the UK to Northern Rock (NR), a building society with its base in Newcastle, when it started running out of cash. You see the problem with NR was that, unlike other banks who get money from customers lodging money on deposit, its business was built around mortgage lending. When other banks would not lend to it, the BOE had to step in and give NR emergency funding. This led to panic from those who had money on deposit with NR. Savers queued in their hundreds outside offices, waiting to withdraw their money and put it somewhere safer. In a matter of days almost £2 billion had been withdrawn from Northern Rock.

Eventually NR was nationalized, which meant the government took over the bank entirely, otherwise it is almost certain that it would have gone bankrupt – something the government did not want to happen.

meltdown monday

Before the problem with Northern Rock happened over in the UK, much worse things were happening in the United States.

Lehman Brothers, which was one of the biggest investment banks in the world, was forced into bankruptcy on Monday 15 September 2008, which is now known as 'Meltdown Monday.'

On the same day, one of their rival banks, Merrill Lynch, which was regarded as one of Wall Street's most distinguished banks, had to be rescued and taken over by Bank of America or also face disaster.

Lehman Brothers filed for bankruptcy because the bank had just lost US $14 billion (that's $14,000,000,000,000) in high-risk property loans.

Lehman Brothers was a major player in the mortgage market in the United States and because of this it faced a greater risk that big losses could – and eventually would – be fatal to them.

To understand this further let me explain how this happened and how and why what has become known as the 'credit crunch' came about.

the credit crunch

The credit crunch began in the United States when mortgage lenders agreed to give mortgages to people who in the past had struggled to meet loan repayments. The banks were aware of the poor credit history of these people but offered them what are called '*subprime loans*' nonetheless. Some lenders gave as much as 100 percent of the purchase price of a property to people with a bad credit history.

They were given these loans at discounted rates so as to make them affordable at the outset. Of course, the problem with this type of lending is that when the discounted period is over your monthly repayment will increase. It was tough enough anyway for mortgage holders in America when this discounted period elapsed, but in the meantime interest rates had also increased a number of times compounding the problem. This resulted in a massive increase in subprime-mortgage holders' monthly repayments with devastating effects.

When the banks were giving out these types of loan they did not have a problem raising the money to do so. They 'bundled' all of their subprime loans together in what was called a '*collateralized debt obligation*' (CDO).

What they did with this CDO was to sell it for cash to another bank, together with the right to receive the mortgage repayments from all those subprime-mortgage holders bundled in the CDO.

Banks continued passing on CDOs, either by selling them outright or by using them as collateral to borrow money.

The deck of cards began to tumble in the summer of 2008 when millions of Americans began falling further and further behind with their mortgage payments. It became impossible to raise money through an equity release scheme on your property as the value of properties was tumbling and people owed more than what their houses were worth. Houses were repossessed by financial institutions and nobody knew how many more mortgage holders would default on their repayments. The housing market collapsed as a result.

In the UK more than 40,000 homes were repossessed in 2008 and it is predicted that this figure will reach 75,000 in 2009 because those people who have lost their jobs may not be able to repay their mortgages.

So, back to what happened to Lehman Brothers and other financial institutions. They had bought what have become known as '*toxic assets*.' These were the bundled loans, which had gone bad, had no value and would never be repaid, so they had to be written off.

Investors and other financial institutions knowing this, believed that Northern Rock, Lehman Brothers and other banks had no value. If investors loaned money to them, they might never get their money back.

if a bank fails is my money safe?

The answer is 'yes' – up to a certain amount.

In the UK, savings providers registered with the Financial Services Authority are all signed up to the Financial Services Compensation Scheme, which guarantees the first £50,000 held with a single institution.

Prior to the problems with Northern Rock the amount guaranteed had been £35,000. If you ever win money or inherit it, place only a maximum of £50,000 with each bank. Tell this to your parents, just in case they don't know.

However, many banks and building societies that operate under separate names are, in fact, owned by a larger bank. If this is the case then you are only protected once. For example, because Lloyds TSB and HBOS have merged, if you had £50,000 with Lloyds and £50,000 with HBOS you are now only covered for one of your £50,000!

So, spread your money around and don't have 'all your eggs in one basket.'

what about building societies?

A building society is similar to a bank except that many are owned by their members, unlike banks which are owned by shareholders. Building Societies offer banking facilities but are more noted for their main business, which is mortgage lending.

The first building society was formed in Birmingham in 1774 and it was set up with one aim in mind – to get money to buy a house for its members. When this was done the building society closed.

Later building societies became what was known as 'permanent', which meant the society would continue on a rolling basis taking in new members when existing ones exited after completing the purchase of a home.

At their height there were hundreds of building societies in the UK and just about every town up and down the land had a building society named after it. Some remain that way today – Coventry Building Society, Barnsley BS, Leeds BS, Nottingham BS to mention but a few.

At the start of 2008 there were 59 building societies in the UK with assets exceeding £36 billion. The number of building societies continues to reduce due to a series of mergers and takeovers brought about by the recent financial crisis.

Building societies actively compete with banks for the majority of banking services and your money is protected up to £50,000 with them, so you should definitely consider building societies when deciding where to place your account.

What is a credit union?

This is an organization made up of people that save together and lend to each other at an affordable rate of interest. It is owned by its members and is often run by volunteers, credit committees (those who approve or deny loan requests) and a board of directors. They all work to represent members' interests in the best way possible.

Every member has an equal say in how the credit union is run, regardless of how much you have in savings. So, someone with £100 and someone with £10,000 would both have an equal say in how their credit union is run.

More and more credit unions are opening up across the UK, and at present about 15,000 people operate their current account from a local credit union. Their popularity is likely to increase over the coming years, particularly as people are very 'anti-bank' at present.

A credit union is used primarily by its members for the purpose of securing a loan, which could be used for a car purchase, home improvement, holiday and so on. It tends to be easier, particularly nowadays, to get money from a credit union rather than a bank.

Credit unions do not offer as broad a range of services as a bank does but some are not far behind. Personally I think credit unions are great because they provide loans at competitive rates, they promote prudence and they have a set of values that include:

* equality, equity and mutual self-help

The differences between credit unions and banks:

credit unions	banks
Owned by members	**Owned by outside shareholders**
Operated by volunteer boards	**Controlled by paid board of directors**
Not-for-profit cooperations	**Owned by shareholders who want profit**

I would recommend that you open an account with your local credit union and save on a regular basis with them. You never know when, in the future, you may want to get a loan, so having an account that you regularly pay into is a great way of building up a good profile and making it easier to get a loan.

A credit union is not a substitute for a bank or building society but that does not mean you should not have an account with one – you should!

online banking

You probably spend a lot of your time online surfing the net, downloading music, chatting with friends on Facebook or a blogger site, and so on, so it's great that you can also do almost all of your banking from the comfort of your Mac or PC at home.

Online banking has become very popular because it is just so convenient and quick. There's no need to travel to your bank branch to check your account balance, no need to wait in queues and – for some online accounts – no need to pay fees. It's also very green as you don't need to have paper bank statements and you can correspond with your bank through its site.

In most cases you can access your account directly through your bank's website. Once you are set up and you have clearance, it will give you the appropriate passwords and login data and you're good to go.

But be smart, be aware!

The majority of banks nowadays use quite a bit of internet protection like firewalls and data encryption to make sure that online thieves can't get access to your personal information, but, alas, no system is fool proof.

So, be vigilant, keep your eyes and ears open for internet scams such as emails from someone pretending to be from your bank. If they ask for personal information do not give it to them. This is a scam called '*phishing*' (pronounced 'fishing'). The sender's address seems to be legitimate and looks as if it is from your bank. The email might say that your bank wants to 'update' or 'validate' personal information such as your user name, password, credit card or bank account number.

If you are suspicious of such emails *DELETE, DELETE, DELETE*.

Make sure no one, apart from perhaps a parent or guardian, knows your access password or pin code and under no circumstances give out any personal information regarding your bank account to anyone online unless it's a secure site that you trust.

identity theft

You obviously don't want anyone to obtain personal information about you and then wrongfully use this to withdraw money from your account or to obtain credit loans, purchases, or anything else, in your name.

Adults are not the only target for fraudsters. They even target children who are too young to have a current account or credit card. What they do is use a name, address and/or national insurance number to open an account.

While I don't want to frighten you, I do want to make sure that you and your family are as protected from ID theft as you can be.

Follow my top 8 tips and that should help you protect yourself.

liam's tips to avoid identity fraud

☑ **buy a shredding machine** –
Shred any document that shows your name, address, bank account numbers and any other information that could provide access to your personal information.

☑ **be careful at atm machines** –
Beware of 'shoulder surfers' behind you who are trying to read your pin number and gain access to your account.

☑ **put passwords on all of your accounts** –
Don't use 'password' or '123456' as your passwords. Make up a fictitious word that combines letters and numbers.

☑ **do not carry unnecessary identification**
Do not put your ATM or credit card pin number in your wallet along with your card. If the wallet or handbag is stolen then you are making it so easy for the thief.

☑ **do not give personal information to a stranger** –
If someone calls you and you do not know them, i.e. they may pretend to be carrying out a 'market survey', never give out or verify personal information. Ask for their number and say you will call them back – they are likely to hang up very quickly and try someone else.

☑ **try to get an atm card with your photo on it** –
Some banks now offer this.

☑ **be aware when buying online** –
Do not use your account number or credit card if you are buying something online unless it is encrypted or on a secure site.

☑ **get an account statement every month** –
Check your statement carefully, whether online or on paper, to see if there is anything on it that you don't recognize.

be savvy - don't get scammed!

Be savvy!

If it sounds too good to be true then it could be and probably is a *SCAM*!

What is a scam? Well it is an unfair attempt to obtain money from you or get your personal details. The internet and mobile phones, in particular, are favourite hunting grounds for scam artists and many of them are now targeting UK teenagers.

some of these scams include:

£ ### expensive ringtone charges that are linked to a subscription service

Mobile users may often receive offers of a free ringtone, games or screensavers. If it is not made clear that in order to get this free ringtone you have to agree to a subscription service then you are being scammed.

£ ### sms scams based on text messaging subscription services

One of the most common scams of late is when you get a text message to your phone asking you to enter a competition or play a game. These messages are charged at premium rates and you could end up with a massive bill if you engage in text conversation with these numbers.

£ ### 0870 lines asking you to claim a prize such as a holiday or an itouch player

... When you haven't even entered a competition? That should give you a heads up but basically these operate on a similar basis to the ringtone or SMS scams. You get a text saying you have won a prize, usually a great one, and in order to claim it you have to reply to a number that is charged at a premium rate.

£ ### unexpected requests for your personal details on social networking sites like bebo and facebook

It is great to make new friends on social networking sites such as Bebo or Facebook, and chat online but these sites are now becoming a prime target for con artists and identity thieves phishing for your personal information.

£ **email from an unknown source asking you to open an attachment**
These attachments can steal your address, passwords and bank account details.

don't panic!

Listen, if you do fall victim to a scam don't panic, but equally don't sit on the problem for too long through embarrassment or whatever, hoping it will miraculously go away because it won't.

Act as soon as you can! So...

• **talk to your parents, a teacher or someone you trust**

• **let your friends know what happened to you so that it doesn't happen to them**

• **take steps to stop the scam, i.e. stop any payment if you can**

chapter 3
credit and loans

Credit cards are a very convenient way to purchase items and they are impossible to do without in the modern world – as so much of our lives revolve around credit, for example, when booking a flight online, a hotel, car hire, or buying things on the web.

However, if they are misused then they are potentially lethal to your finances!

Credit card companies do not give you credit cards because of their generosity of spirit. They give them to you because they want you to use them in a way that makes them money by charging interest. Hundreds of thousands of people, of course, do just that because they either do not repay the total amount each month, just pay off interest, or fail to make a payment on time or at all.

I often hear people say that the day they got into serious financial difficulty was the day that they got their first credit card. The problem, though, is that most people believe the burden of responsibility lies with the credit card company and not with them. But this is not how it's seen in the real world.

Now card companies deserve some blame with their clever marketing, gold and platinum cards, increased credit limits and so on, but the real responsibility for controlling our debt lies with us – and we know it!

The amount we, as a nation, owed in credit card debt in February 2009 was £53 billion. The average credit card limit in the UK per person is £5,129.

how credit card debt grows

Once you get a card, usually with a limit of around £1,000 minimum, it is all too easy to use it – and to do so without keeping a track of how much you are spending.

Practically every shop we go into invites us to spend, whether we have cash in our wallets or not.

Sometimes we have four weeks' delay from the time we make our purchase to the day we get our bill. When the bill does come in you may have forgotten about that lunch, those shoes, those concert tickets, and so there is no way for you to settle the bill in full – at least not *this month*.

That is how the debt crisis begins.

You start to make only the minimum payment each month, which covers the interest and nothing else – the principle debt remains.

People think, '*Well, I paid the amount they asked me for on time, so aren't I a responsible card holder?*'

You certainly are – from the credit card company's point of view. They love customers who pay the minimum amount each month.

Why? Because the balance that is carried forward into the next month accrues more interest!

Until the credit crunch, less scrupulous credit card issuers often increased the borrower's limit in these cases, without that person even asking – and so debt spiralled out of control.

The minimum payment on a credit card is normally a certain percentage on the outstanding debt, normally between 2 percent and 3 percent with a minimum payment of £10.

Let me give you an example of the real cost of purchases if you only pay back the minimum amount each month:

Item	Purchase Price (£)	Years it will take to pay off with minimum payments	Total Interest Paid (£)	Total cost (£)
Stereo	**500**	**7**	**367**	**867**
Computer	**1000**	**13**	**1129**	**2,129**

So, you see this is the problem with minimum repayments. People often complain that they seem to be getting nowhere and they are right. Can you imagine how long it would take to repay the sum in full if the debt was even higher than that shown in the table? Just £5,000 would take you 22 years to repay – yes 22 years! So, if you were 18 years old and owed £5,000 you would be 40 before you cleared it!

The average interest rate on credit card lending in the UK is 17.92 percent, which is 17.5 percent above the Bank of England base rate. Madness! Yet, on average, 235 plastic card purchases were made in the UK every second in 2008.

liam's tips for using a credit card responsibly

☑ **limit the number of cards you have**
Fewer cards make it easier to track the amounts you owe, repayment dates, etc.

☑ **avoid store cards**
Unless you repay the amount due each month – because store cards tend to charge higher interest rates than normal cards.

☑ **pay off the balance in full each month**
Spend only what you can afford to pay for that month – set a budget.

☑ **cut your own limit**
If you are worried, then cut your own limit.

good housekeeping

And here are some tips for managing your credit card account:

☑ **set up a direct debit from your account to pay the full amount due each month**

☑ **keep your pin safe at all times**

☑ **keep a record of your monthly statements**

☑ **find out what interest rate you are being charged**

☑ **don't use the card for expensive purchases that you can't pay off immediately – term loans are cheaper**

A word of caution – if you set up a direct debit to pay off your credit card, you must be sure of funds in your account. You may not be allowed to go overdrawn if you don't have an overdraft. If this is the case then the direct debit will not pay the amount to your visa.

credit card fraud

As long as there are cards there will always be attempts at credit card fraud.

Tips to help you avoid fraud:

Only give out security information on your credit card, like your mother's maiden name, accounts passwords, etc., on calls that you initiate.

Monitor your monthly bill closely when it arrives and make sure that any new transactions were made by you or an authorized user on the account.

Report suspicions of fraud to your credit card company immediately using a trusted number.

Report lost or stolen cards immediately.

Finally, remember that if you do not repay the amount owed on time every month you are taking out a loan at a very high rate of interest. Think about this every time you consider using your card.

If you didn't have a credit card and someone offered you a loan of £50 to buy a new pair of jeans would you take it from them? Of course you wouldn't! So adopt that same attitude towards your credit card and you will be fine.

what is a debit card?

A debit card is a one which deducts money from your current account just like an ATM card. So every time you use it, money is subtracted from what money you already have. Be warned though – if you have no money in your account then using your card will take you overdrawn. Your bank will charge you a fee for going overdrawn and then a high rate of interest on the outstanding debit. Always be aware of the amount of money in your account and do not spend more than this limit.

what about a store card?

A store card is yet another form of credit card offered by particular stores and even by football teams. If you use it to purchase items in their store or online you will get discounts, be offered promotions, get invitations to special launches, etc. Don't get sucked into this, whatever you do! The rate of interest is often very high, higher than normal credit cards, so don't use it just because you will get a discount on goods, unless you are absolutely certain that you are going to repay the debt on time.

so, what's a prepaid card?

A prepaid credit card is not actually a credit card since no credit is being offered to you. However, it may carry a brand like Visa, MasterCard or Discover and can be used as though it was a regular credit card. The prepaid credit card is a growing industry in the UK. Consumers are at last realizing the dangers of credit cards and how much trouble they can get into with a credit limit.

It works by someone opening an account for a fee, transferring money into the account and then you can start using the card. It lies somewhere between a debt and credit card. Much like phone top-up cards or gift cards in a department store, you can never overspend because the card simply won't let you. It can be used where ever visa or mastercards are accepted.

There is a transaction fee every time you use the card to purchase something and some cards may carry a monthly fee. The great thing with a prepaid credit card is that the amount you spend on it is determined by you and by how much you put on the card. Prepaid cards allow up to about £500 and no more on your account at any one time. With a prepaid card you can purchase anything where credit cards are accepted.

Prepaid cards are ideal for teenagers and young adults, particularly for shopping online. They give you freedom as you don't constantly have to keep getting your parents' card/s to complete your transaction/s.

how can i apply for a loan?

Suppose you and your mates decide to head off for a two-week holiday or you decide you want to buy a car but you don't have the money to pay for it in cash, what do you do? Either you do without or you have to take out a loan.

Now just because you have an account with a particular bank it does not mean that they will treat you any different to those who don't and equally it does not mean you should only go to them for the loan. You should, of course, *SHOP AROUND* first for a lender that offers the best deal.

Search the internet for lenders. There are a wealth of online resources available to you from the comfort of your armchair. Sometimes car companies, for example, offer low interest or even zero interest rate loans when you purchase one of their cars.

So, your first step before you even book that holiday or put a deposit on that car is to find out how much you can afford to borrow and whether a lender will give you the amount needed.

You are not going to know this until you make an application to them.

They will want to know the following from you:

☑ **name, address, telephone number**

☑ **how much you earn**

☑ **how long you have worked in your current job – this could be a part-time job by the way**

- ☑ **how much money you owe on other loans**

- ☑ **who you bank with**

- ☑ **your national insurance number**

They will then evaluate your application and decide if you are a 'good risk' or not. They will want to be as certain as they can be that you will be able to pay them back. The bank will find out whether:

- ☑ **you earn enough to keep up with the repayments**

- ☑ **you have a history of paying your debts on time**

- ☑ **you 'manage' your money well each month – they may want to have a look at your current account statements**

They will also contact a credit bureau and ask for a report, which is basically a summary of your repayment habits.

After weighing up all of this information, the bank will then either approve or refuse your loan request.

Before you apply for a loan:

- ☑ **Ask yourself, 'would I lend to myself?'– and then answer honestly – look at how much you earn, what you want the money for, what your credit rating is like, whether you operate your accounts well (are you always overdrawn or do you have a surplus each month).**

- ☑ **Do your homework –**
Apply to a bank that would fight with others to give you money. This will lead to cheaper interest rates for you and quicker decisions when applying.

Finally, *don't ever overborrow!*

Find out in advance how much, for example, £1,000 is going to cost you each month and never pay more than 30 percent of what you earn each month on loans. If you go past this figure you are heading for trouble.

different types of loan

Below is a guide to the rates of interest usually charged for different types of loan:

lender	typical rate of interest %
Banks/Building Societies	
Special student packages	0
Increase over agreed limit	5–8
Unauthorized borrowing	20–30
Finance houses	11–16
Credit cards	10–20
Credit unions	10–27
Store cards	15–30
Licensed 'non-standard' lenders	50–100
Loan sharks	*whatever they want! Avoid!*

what is my credit rating?

I mentioned that a bank will do a credit check on you before they give you any money. This is actually a good idea on their part because it shows them how you repaid loans in the past. The report will tell them if you have repaid loans on time all of the time or whether you went into arrears for one, two or even three months.

Whether you get the loan or not will depend on how good or bad your credit rating is. If you do get a loan, it will also determine the rate of interest.

If your credit rating is good and you have a history of repaying loans on time then a bank will be very keen to give you money. If you have a history of constantly missing repayments then they will not be so eager and if they do reluctantly give you money, boy are they going to charge you for it.

People make the mistake of being lazy about how they pay back their loans. They think it is OK to miss one or two repayments as they will catch up at some stage. They don't realize that a bank views it completely differently. From their point of view you are unable to pay back the loan. And if this is the case, how are you going to repay the new loan they might give you? Do they really want the hassle of chasing you every month with letters and phone calls asking you to bring your account up to date? Not really.

Now let me tell you what the impact of having a bad credit rating is. It means:

- you will never get a loan from anyone again (this includes overdrafts, mortgages, and so on)
- if you do, you will be charged a much higher rate of interest because you are perceived as 'high risk' by the bank

---

Let me tell you a true story.

Two friends bought a house near one another. The price of the houses was the same and they borrowed the same amount of money. One guy had a good repayment history and the other didn't. He had had a loan a couple of years ago and he had paid it off in full, but he was always two or three repayments behind.

The guy with the good repayment history borrowed £225,000 at 3.4 percent, which meant his monthly repayment over 25 years was £1,114 per month.

His friend with the poor repayment history borrowed the same amount over the same term but because he was a greater risk, he was charged a rate of 7.4 percent. His monthly repayment was £1,648 per month.

The difference between what these two friends were repaying was £534 each month or £6,408 each year.

All negative information about your past loans can stay on credit bureau records for between 1 to 6 years.

---

student loans

If you are thinking about going to university in the future then you have got to think about how you are going to pay for it.

Along with choosing your course and college, you will have to consider tuition fees and the cost of covering your living expenses.

Unless money is no object for your Mum and/or Dad you may have to consider taking out a loan to get yourself through college.

Before I get into the whole area of borrowing money, let me mention that there is financial support available from the government that will help you with the costs you are going to encounter.

Preparing and finding out well in advance what you are and are not entitled to will mean one less thing to distract you from focusing on your course.

By the way, did you know that graduates tend to earn 20–25 percent more than those without a degree? So, in the long run you will be better off by going to university.

government loans

You can take out two loans from the government, which will help with:

1. **tuition fees**

2. **maintenance fees (accommodation and other living expenses)**

Many students mistakenly believe that these facilities are a gift of some sort that don't really have to be repaid. Well wake up and smell the coffee – they are loans that have to be repaid at some stage. Repayment kicks in when:

• **you have left/completed your course, and**

• **you start earning over £15,000 per year**

Once you start earning above £15,000 each year, you will pay back at a rate of about 9 percent interest on whatever amount you earn in excess of £15,000.

So, if you leave college and start earning £20,000 per year, you will start with repayments of £450 in the first year, that is: £5,000 x 9% = £450.

You pay a little bit of interest on your loans but the amount you borrow is about the same as you repay.

If you do get a student loan and you are not due to start making repayments until 2012 you can actually take a repayment break on this loan of up to 5 years!

maintenance grant

This maintenance grant is for living expenses and it is available to help students entering college, especially those from poorer backgrounds, with their day-to-day living costs.

In England and Wales those eligible can get a grant of up to £2,765 or £3,265 if you live in Northern Ireland.

Statistics show that about a third of all new students will qualify for this full maintenance grant and another third again will qualify for a partial grant.

You can also get what is called a 'bursary payment', which is an extra source of help from the college or university you are going to attend. If you are getting the full maintenance grant then you almost certainly can expect a bursary payment as well.

Remember grants and bursary payments do not have to be repaid!

So, the moral of this story is find out what you're entitled to as there may be financial help available of which you're not aware.

liam's tips for helping students/new students

£ try and estimate how much money you will need each week

£ for full-time students the quickest and easiest way to apply for loans or grants is to go online and research

£ if you are a new full-time student you can apply for finance as soon as you have applied for the course of your choice – fill in your Local Authority (LA) form (called a PN1 for new students) because if you don't, it will stop you from obtaining a student loan

£ if you want to apply for financial help after your course has started you must do so within nine months from the first day of the academic year for your course

how do i get a mortgage?

Buying a home is the single biggest financial commitment most people will ever make in their lifetime. In most cases a mortgage is a long-term commitment, so selecting the right mortgage lender and product is crucial.

Much like getting a credit card or car loan you should shop around to see who is offering the best value in the market, compare how much each bank is willing to lend, what repayments options are available and so on. This means that when you make that big decision as to who you are going to place your business with, it is an informed one, as you will have considered the merits of each lender.

Arranging a mortgage to purchase your new property can be a daunting task. Where do you start? And more importantly how do you ensure that the mortgage you choose is the best one for you?

Typically each lending institution will have standard lending criteria, that will have to be adhered to before they will entertain a loan application. Some of these include the following:

☑ **age 18 or over**

☑ **continuous permanent employment for a minimum of six months**

☑ **property being purchased or used as security is located in the United Kingdom**

☑ **maximum age on completion of the loan is 65/70, depending on your lender**

☑ **whether applicants may be subject to work or visa permit restrictions**

☑ **good credit history**

The above list are just some samples of the criteria required by lenders and will vary from lender to lender.

You can arrange your mortgage from a variety of different sources. Deciding which one you will choose should be based upon:

- **the amount they are willing to lend to you**

- **how competitive they are**

- **customer service**

- **flexibility, i.e. overpayments, underpayments, interest only facilities, extension of term, mortgage breaks, etc.**

- **fees, if any**

- **reputation – do you know anyone who may have used that particular lender or broker before and what was their experience like with them**

subprime mortgages

I mentioned earlier that one of the minimum criteria set by mainstream banks before they will give you any money to buy anything (let alone a house!) is that you have a good credit history.

If you don't, your only option could be a subprime mortgage – and, you really don't want one of these.

Remember the example of the two friends who bought the same house and borrowed the same amount of money but had different repayment histories. The difference between their monthly repayments was huge. That is the consequence of having a poor repayment history – you are going to be charged very high rates of interest!

You will see in the newspapers or on TV that interest rates are at an all time low and that the Bank of England has reduced rates to .5 percent. This is great if you have a good repayment history, but not if you have a subprime mortgage because interest on these is still being charged at 6–7 percent.

If you take just one thing from this book, please let it be how to repay loans now and in the future. Always repay them on time all of the time, otherwise you will pay for it later by being refused credit or by paying a very high rate of interest.

What is negative equity?

'Negative equity' means that you owe your lender more than what your house is worth.

If, for example, you got a 100 percent mortgage from a mortgage lender to purchase a property, which means that you got a mortgage equal to the purchase price of the property.

If the sales value of your house then falls, which is what has happened in the UK over the past two years, you are in negative equity.

> **Let's say, for example, that you bought a property costing £160,000 in 2007 and you borrowed the full amount from your bank. The property has fallen in value and is now only worth £130,000. You still owe £160,000 but if you went to sell the house in the morning you would only get £130,000, so you have a negative equity problem of £30,000.**

The number of people estimated to be in a negative equity situation in the UK is 1.3 MILLION! And this could – and probably does – include someone you know, whether it be your own parent/s, siblings or friends. If it's your parents they may be affected by many of the things I have discussed in the previous and following chapters.

Some people believe that the value of property could fall by between 30–50 percent of what it was worth just over two years ago!

How do you prevent this happening to you in the future? The answer is twofold:

1. **don't ever borrow 100 percent of the purchase price of a property**
   This leaves you much more open to falling into a negative equity trap. Save as much as you can towards the purchase. If you buy a property costing £160,000 but you have saved £20,000, you are now only borrowing £140,000. This reduces your exposure to negative equity in a big way.

2. **take your time when buying property**
   Don't rush out and buy anything just to get on the 'property ladder'. This is the mistake many people made, they thought prices would keep going up and up and if they didn't buy now then they would miss out. Well, if people didn't buy in the past couple of years and didn't borrow a 100 percent mortgage, the only thing they are missing out on is negative equity.

chapter 4
the economy

what is the economy?

An 'economy' is a system made up of producing, exchanging and distributing goods and services within a city (local economy), a country (national economy) and the world as a whole (international economy).

The people or companies that make and provide these goods/services are called 'producers', and the people who buy and use these goods/services are called 'consumers'.

Of course, most consumers are producers as well. For example, if a person works for Apple Macintosh computers and helps to assemble a computer they are producers. If they buy a computer from iMac for their own personal use, then they are consumers.

The economy, therefore, is that essential link between consumers and producers and how they work together using human and natural resources to produce the goods that people want and need.

natural resources

Any material or substance that occurs in nature, which can be exploited for economic gain (that is, it has an economic value) is known as a 'natural resource'. Examples of such substances or materials include gold, timber, fresh water and scenery that attracts tourists.

For many countries – and regions within countries – the location of natural resources will often determine the kind of work, or industry, that is carried out in that area.

making the most of what you've got

The local economies of some of the mountainous regions in Austria, Italy, Switzerland and France are dominated by the tourist industry. These countries have developed excellent skiing facilities, taking advantage of the mountains' natural ski slopes. These areas receive an abundance of snow, so why wouldn't they take advantage of this natural resource?

The same can be said of countries that have a warm, sunny climate throughout the year, such as Egypt or India. They use this to their advantage by actively persuading tourists to come and visit them, which means that their economies are also largely based on tourist industries.

So, for many countries the type of activity for which they are known, and which they exploit for economic gain, is often based on a local natural resource, be it beautiful countryside, weather, snow, coal or fish.

it's a case of supply and demand!

Let's look at consumers and producers a little more closely and at how they interact as this is key to the working of an economy. Do you ever wonder why shops charge a different price for the same product? Each shop owner sets out his or her own prices but we, the consumers, help them when they make their decisions.

If there is a demand from the consumer for a particular good or service but there is a shortage of that good (*the supply*) then the price for that good will, all things being equal, go up as *demand exceeds supply*. People will pay more to get this good because of its scarceness and both the seller and the producer knows this.

When there is a huge amount of stock for a good available and the demand from consumers is not so great, or if there are several shops selling the same item, then all of that is likely to push the price down as *supply exceeds demand*.

Let's look at this in action.

A couple of years ago in the UK there was a massive demand for property. However, there was a problem, as not enough new houses were being built to cater for that demand from consumers. So, the problem was essentially a shortage of houses. People were willing to pay increasing amounts of money to buy property, so the asking prices increased significantly to often overly inflated prices.

Nowadays, the number of people buying houses has dropped – partly because of these prices and partly because of the credit crunch. With the number of houses available to buy now greater than the number of purchasers, this has led to a sharp drop in house prices in most areas.

the knock-on effect

Demand and supply in one particular sector of the economy often affects what happens to another.

For example, if people were able to read their favourite newspapers for free online, then fewer people might actually buy those newspapers. As a result some newsagents might close and ink manufacturers and paper suppliers might have to reduce the cost of ink and paper or make redundancies.

Let's look at another business affected by supply and demand. With so many movie channels now available to view in the comfort of your own home and DVD companies that deliver straight to your door, what effect do you think this has had on DVD rental shops? Obviously not as many people are renting DVDs from these stores anymore.

Many rental outlets have responded to this by diversifying (changing, altering or broadening) their offerings. Along with being able to rent a DVD you can now rent game consoles and games, buy a mobile phone, and so on, in rental shops.

So DVD shops have responded to demand for DVDs dropping off, but rather than seeking to increase or decrease prices they looked at alternative ways to attract new customers, possibly from different age groups, by offering new products that might potentially generate sales for them and earn new income.

The ability to adapt to changing circumstances is important no matter what your business endeavour is, or your age. It is important in keeping you one step ahead of the competition and also helps you monitor your financial position closely.

is our economy working well?

It is quite easy to know if your business is doing well or not, as essentially, you are either making a *profit* or a *loss*.

But, how do we know if our economy is doing well or not? Basically through what economists tell us. An *'economist'* is a person who studies the economy and he or she looks at all sorts of information to see how well or badly an economy is performing. These are just a few of the questions he or she might ask:

£ **are the prices of goods and services increasing or decreasing?**

£ **what is the country's rate of unemployment?**

£ **what is the rate of inflation?**

what is inflation? and why is it important?

You might think that it would be great if everyone had lots of money to spend, *spend, spend, spend*. It does sound great but when this does happen and when lots of people are buying things the result is *inflation*.

Put simply, inflation is when the goods or services you buy (that iPod, for example) costs more than they used to – they have increased or 'inflated' in price. How does this relate to you?

If, for example, you bought an iPod in January for £200 and six months later the same iPod costs £210, that's the result of inflation.

If there is lots of money in the economy and people are willing to spend more for a good than before, retailers will become aware of this and will increase their prices as they will still sell the same amount as they had before but for more profit, unless their costs have also risen.

I am sure you will often see or hear on the news, or read on the net, that '*the current rate of inflation is*' or '*inflation rose by.*' Inflation is talked about because it's another way of measuring how our economy is performing – how well or badly the supply of goods is meeting demand from the consumer.

If the supply of a particular good is equal to demand by the consumer then there will be little or no inflation.

However, if there is an increase in demand for the product by the consumer or, if it costs more to produce the good, then prices will usually increase.

hard times for us all

Inflation can be difficult for us all – not just your parents, but you, as well. Why?

The real value of your pound will decrease in times of high inflation. What you might have bought for £2 yesterday (a smoothie, for example) might cost you £4 today, which means that your money is worth less today than it was yesterday because it now takes twice as much money to buy the same thing.

People also find that when inflation is high their salaries do not tend to increase as fast as prices, so even if you get a pay rise it mightn't be enough to keep up with price increases.

Here is something to ask your friends or parents – have they seen the cost of their weekly shopping increase over the past year, even though they are more or less buying the same things? If they say '*yes*', well that shows inflation at work for you.

what is a recession?

OK, so you have your eye on a new game console and you are saving hard to buy it. But suppose that each week the cost of that console is increasing more than the amount you are managing to save each week. What do you think would happen if this was occurring right across the country? People would have less money, or less '*disposable income*' to spend on goods and services, and those items would remain unsold or unused.

If fewer goods are being sold then a manufacturer will make fewer of them, which will lead to fewer workers being needed to produce them – and unemployment will rise as a result.

Let's take the example of building houses again. If fewer people are buying because they have less money or they can't get loans from banks, then fewer houses will be sold, resulting in builders working at a slower pace, if they are able to find work at all, as the construction of fewer houses means that not as many workers will be needed in that industry.

All of these things may cause a *recession*, which is when the demand for goods slows, unemployment rises and there is less money in the economy to spend. And, this is what is happening in the UK today. Britain has officially entered recession for the first time since 1991 and our economy has fallen by the biggest margin since 1980.

A recession will typically last for a period of two years or less, but if it lasts longer it could turn into what's called a '*depression*', which is what many people are currently saying has happened to our economy.

this is depressing!

When a depression happens prices drop because there are just too many goods for sale and no one has the money to buy them. So, people will sell their goods and services for much less money than before rather than not sell them at all. This is why some shops seem to have permanent sales. For example, a good which might normally cost £5 may drop as low as 50 pence in price during a period of depression. And, this obviously has a knock-on effect on other areas. Unemployment tends to rise greatly during a depression and people are prepared to work for very little money just to put food on the table, pay bills or keep a roof over their heads.

Back in 1929 the United States experienced what is now known as the Great Depression, which lasted for most of the 1930s and resulted in 13 million people unemployed.

What helped the United States out of this depression? The outbreak of the Second World War (1939–45) in Europe.

Yes, a world war helped get the country's economy going again by producing demand for essential goods and services. With many food supply routes cut off, America had to fend for itself, domestically producing food and equipment for its own people and then its own troops when it entered the war in 1941.

With men leaving the workforce to join up and serve their country abroad, women stepped in to do the work. More than 5 million of them entered the workplace, employed on farms, in factories and other places to produce vital food and equipment needed to keep the country and its troops going. Women in the workplace are now commonplace but at that time, such numbers were revolutionary.

Generally, the creation of demand for goods and services, whether it be through a war, or through other methods, helps countries to recover from economic depressions. Other help can come through government spending on essential services.

where does our government get money to run the country?

What our governments spend on the nation is also important.

The next time you are walking down the street, start to take notice of the roads, trees, schools, hospitals and libraries.

You may take them a bit for granted. They are just there but their standard and quality – a smooth pavement instead of a cracked or broken one that may cause you to fall over and crack a tooth – depends on the money invested in them by governments and local authorities. But where does this money come from?

You and your families help by paying 'taxes', which is money a government collects from individuals and businesses, whether through income or council tax or through hidden taxes such as value added taxes (VAT) on the goods you buy. In turn, the government will use this collected money, along with money they borrow, to help pay for these essential services.

how much does the government need to collect?

Well this is a tricky one. Just exactly how does a government of any country decide how much tax people or companies should pay?

First of all they need to look at two things:

1. **how much money they need**

2. **how much people can afford to give them**

It's as simple as that.

The government will make a *budget* (forecast) estimating how much money it will need to run the country for, say, the next three years. It then must decide how much of this money can be collected in taxes and how much it might need to borrow.

It is quite a balancing act because if it sets the taxes too high then people will have less money to spend on goods and services, yet, if it sets taxes too low then it will not have enough money to spend on key public goods and services such as schools, new roads, hospitals, and so on.

So, money needed to run a country essentially comes from two sources:

1. **borrowing**

2. **taxes**

borrowing

Governments get most of their money by taxing people who live within their country. However, the amount needed by a government and the amount it spends is far greater than the amount of money available to it through taxes. So, in order to bridge the difference, it needs to borrow money, and that is how nations start accruing debt. This debt comes from funding wars overseas, health care, social security payments and any other government-provided services and securities.

The government debt or *national debt* is the total amount outstanding on last year's – and all of its other years' – borrowing requirements.

It borrows the money by printing and selling what are called '*gilt-edged securities*', which are also known as *bonds* and *treasury bills*. They are just pieces of paper, a bit like an IOU, which promise a return of the money borrowed with interest some time in the future. These securities are offered at various times during the year if the government needs to raise more money.

So who buys these bonds/gilts?

They are bought by individuals, insurance companies, pension funds and banks. The government takes the money raised by these 'sales' and then uses the money to spend on its public projects.

When non-banks buy these bonds from governments the money they use is '*saved money*', which is being recycled back into the economy through government spending. Banks, on the other hand, create '*new money*' to buy these government bonds.

The bonds that people buy from the government have a maturity date. This means that the government has to repay them at a particular time in the future. When that happens the government has to find the money to repay them in full. This is also known as '*paying the interest on the national debt*'.

By the way we pay **£27 billion** in interest each year on the money we borrow!

our taxes

Individuals also pay taxes in one form or another. The main forms of tax in the UK are income tax – a tax paid on income – and sales tax or value added tax (VAT), as mentioned earlier in this chapter.

Just because you are not working does not mean you will escape paying income tax. For example, you might have some income from savings that is taxed.

There is no minimum age at which a person has to start paying tax, what matters is the amount of your income.

In the UK 20 pence in every £1 you earn up to £34,800 goes to the government and above this figure every 40p in every £1 you earn goes to the government.

As I have said already, the government uses this money to support and pay for services. I was once asked why we couldn't pay individually just for the services we use? A good question and a fair point, but the reason is that we just couldn't afford to do that and also each person would have to pay a full fee for the service regardless of his or her *ability to pay*.

And it is this ability to pay that most tax systems in democratic countries around the world are based on – put simply, the more we earn, the more taxes we pay as a percentage of our earnings and the opposite is also true, if our incomes are low – the smaller the income, the lower the amount paid as a percentage of earnings.

So, how much goes on each household?

About £8,720 is spent each year on every man, woman and child in the UK, which breaks down to about £58.90 per week on health, £53.60 per week on education and training, £23.20 on policing, public order and safety, and just over £14 on transport.

national insurance

In addition to paying income tax on what you earn, you also have to pay National Insurance contributions (NICs) if you are over 16 years of age, assuming your earnings are above a certain amount. The amount you have to pay is based on what you earn and whether you work for a business or for yourself. You will pay NICs until you retire – currently at 65 for men and 60 for woman. These payments build up your entitlement to certain social security benefits, including the state pension when you retire – such as it is.

If, for example, you are made redundant or you can't work for a period of time due to illness or injury you are able to claim a payment from the government. This payment comes from your NICs.

If you are an employee and earn between £110 and £844 each week then you pay 11 percent of this amount. This could be less if you are a member of your company's pension scheme.

If you are self-employed then you have to make 'class 2' contributions – a flat amount per week of £2.40. So, the benefits that you are entitled to and the amount you can get, will depend on how much and for how long you have been paying your NICs. These include:

- **jobseekers allowance**

- **incapacity benefit – when you can't work due to illness or injury**

- **state pension**

- **widowed parent's allowance**

- **bereavement allowance and payment**

The government uses money from taxes, borrowing and NICs to contribute to some of the areas found in the following table:

government sector	amount (£ billions)
Pensions	65
Social services	24
Health	90
Transport	18
Education and training	70
Defence	31
Industry, agriculture employment and training	24
Recreation, culture and sport	11
Housing and the environment	18
Public order and safety	30
Debt interest	27
Source: money.uk.msn.com, 12 March 2007	

chapter 5
brillant ideas and entrepreneurs

The 'wacky world of business' is sometimes a strange one, where businesses you have never heard of – and which some would say are insane – start up and then make their founder rich. But how does someone become an *entrepreneur* and turn his or her ideas/dreams into reality?

Before I start talking about what an entrepreneur does and how you can become one, let me give you some examples of brilliant business ideas:

A company was set up in New York City called NewYourKey. For a small fee this company will keep a copy of your house or car key in a secure storage facility and will deliver the key straight away if you find yourself locked out. On the way home from a nightclub and can't find your keys? No problem, NewYourKey will deliver spare keys within an hour any time, day or night, wherever a customer happens to be.

What a great and simple idea.

Peasy.com is a UK company that allows people to search online for parking spaces before they leave home. So, if you own a car park space you could start earning money from it by adding it to the peasy network. You give them your details, where your car park space is, when it is available and whether it can be rented weekly or monthly or both.

This company identified the need people have to secure parking before they set out on their journey. Market research found that parking in London, for example, is so difficult that people would book a space before they left home if they could.

How is that for a great business idea?

Another great idea might be:

> Create a deck of cards featuring exercise routines, call them FitDeck and sell the pack online from $9.95. Former Navy SEAL and fitness instructor Phil Black reported sales last year of $4.7 million!

Thomas Edison (1847–1921), the entrepreneur famous for inventing the light bulb, once said, 'I *never perfected an invention that I did not think about in terms of service it might give others ... I find out what the world needs, then I proceed to invent it*.'

That is being an entrepreneur!

how to be an entrepreneur

An entrepreneur is an individual who – rather than working as an employee (someone who works for an employer) – runs a business and assumes all of the risk and, also, the rewards from a given business venture, idea or good or service offered for sale.

An entrepreneur is commonly seen as a business leader and innovator of new ideas.

Entrepreneurs play an incredibly pivotal role in our economy – they have the skills, vision and initiative necessary to take good ideas to the market and then make the ideas profitable.

Let's take a look at three examples of leading entrepreneurs – Sir Richard Branson, Ben Cohen and Jerry Greenfield (Ben & Jerry's) and Mark Zuckerberg, the man behind Facebook.

1. sir richard branson

Whether it is in business or when breaking world records, Sir Richard Branson (b. 1950) probably does it better than anyone else.

Sir Richard built an empire of over 200 companies, employing more than 25,000 people.

But how did he do it? The answer is simply:

 he delivered old products and services in new ways.

 he focused on sectors in which the customer was poorly treated and simply treated them better.

Sir Richard's first business ventures were not very successful – growing Xmas trees and raising budgies – but by the age of 20 he had started a small mail-order record retailer called Virgin.

Sir Richard initially travelled to France to purchase cheap records and then sold them from the trunk of his car and via mail-order. He began to make a profit, as he was able to successfully undercut prices at other record stores in the UK, and, soon afterwards, he opened a shop on Oxford Street, in London.

Over the following years, Sir Richard signed revolutionary and cult acts such as the Sex Pistols and the Rolling Stones to his label, which was fast becoming a world-renowned brand name.

Sir Richard diversified into other markets such as airlines, high-tech trains, mobile phones, soft drinks, book publishing and even a plan to bring people into suborbital space!

As US statesman, Benjamin Franklin (1706–90), once said '*the harder I work the luckier I get*', something that can be applied to Sir Richard, who had the guts, vision, enthusiasm and determination to make his businesses successful.

2. ben cohen & jerry greenfield – the men behind the ice cream

When you say 'Ben & Jerry's', everyone knows you are talking about ice cream.

Ben Cohen and Jerry Greenfield are childhood friends, both born in 1951, in New York.

Ice cream, it seems, was in Ben's blood, as he drove an ice cream van in his senior year of high school.

Ben and Jerry wanted to set up a business, but their first thought was to start a bagel-making business. The equipment was too expensive and so, instead, they settled on the idea of setting up an ice-cream business and went on an ice-cream making course for the princely sum of $5 (£3).

They decided that a great place for an ice-cream parlour was Burlington, Vermont, because no parlour existed there at the time. In 1978, they opened their first shop in a converted petrol station.

The parlour cost a total of $12,000 to buy – Ben and Jerry used $9,000 of their own savings and borrowed a further $4,000 to invest in their new business venture.

They came up with alternative flavours with memorable names, such as Cherry Garcia (frozen yoghurt with cherries and dark chocolate chunks) , the Chunky Monkey (banana ice-cream with chocolate chunks and walnuts) and Jamaican Me Crazy (chunky pineapple sorbet with passionfruit swirls), which were – and are – completely different from the usual chocolate or strawberry flavours on sale.

Ben and Jerry also believed that in order to be successful they needed to connect with their local community. They started to sponsor a free film festival and gave away scoops of ice cream on the anniversary of their first opening – a tradition that continues to this very day.

Ten years after they opened, they were named 'US Small Business Persons of the Year' by Ronald Reagan (1911–2004; President of the United States,1981–9) and by the end of that year they had shops in 18 states in the US. Today, they are an internationally known brand.

In 2000, Ben and Jerry sold their brand for a whopping $326 million – not bad for two guys who initially spent $5 (£3) on an ice-cream making course.

This just shows their entrepreneurial spirit paid off:

☑ **they saw an opportunity**

☑ **took some risks**

☑ **listened to their customers and, most importantly,**

☑ **delivered to them exactly what they wanted.**

3. mark zuckerberg
- the man behind facebook

Mark Zuckerberg (b. 1984), at the age of 19, had a vision and delivered on it. From his dorm room at Harvard University, in 2004, he launched 'Facebook', initially as a campus social-networking system, which later expanded to other colleges.

What happened next was incredible!

The site exploded nationally and then globally. It now has more than 70 million active users.

Zuckerberg's website is the 6th most trafficked site in the US and 1 percent of all internet time is spent on Facebook. It also rates as the No.1 photo-sharing site on the web with over 6 million pictures uploaded every day.

Facebook is now considered to be so valuable that Microsoft paid US$240 million for a 1.6 percent share of it, suggesting it is worth US$15 billion. Not bad for a business that was set up in a dorm room.

so, what do all these entrepreneurs have in common?

☑ **passion**

☑ **commitment**

☑ **risk takers**

☑ **working for themselves**

☑ **guts**

☑ **vision**

In a *BusinessWeek* interview, one businessman said that to be successful you have to '*work hard, be patient and be a sponge while learning your business. Learn how to take criticism. Follow your gut instincts and don't compromise.*' That about sums it all up for me – and, thank you, Simon Cowell for your fantastic words of wisdom.

protecting your idea from those dragons

If you have an idea about a novel new service or an innovative product then how do you ensure that no one steals it? How can you protect it if, for example, you approach a large company with it?

Well, first of all, you are right to be cautious! Last year a woman sued *Victoria's Secret* (the multi-million US lingerie business), claiming they had rejected her pitch to them for an innovative new bra but had allegedly gone on to mass-produce it themselves. What made the bra so different and appealing? It could be worn 100 ways!

While most cases are not like this one, allegations of stolen intellectual property are, unfortunately, quite common.

In the popular TV show, *Dragons' Den*, you might often hear Peter Jones say, '*Great idea but what's to stop me from doing exactly the same thing?*' In some cases, absolutely nothing.

Some people are willing to take this risk because of the benefits of securing a partnership with a bigger corporation or individual who could help them refine, expand and market their idea.

The main reasons that many people 'pitch' their ideas to the 'Dragons' is for their expertise, knowledge and contacts – money, in fact, comes a poor second.

Anyway, back to your ideas! In legal terms, ownership of an idea often belongs to the first person to come up with the idea rather than the first to patent it.

how do you start?

- create an 'inventor's notebook' that details how you developed your idea
- have someone with no stake in your invention sign each page to certify that he or she understands your process. This documents your invention's timeline
- use the copyright symbol © on everything you send out

patents, copyright and trademarks

Don't let somebody get credit for, and profit from, your brilliant ideas.
Safeguard your concepts and inventions.

patent

*This confers upon its holder, for a limited period, the right to exclude others
from exploiting (making, using, selling, importing) the patented invention,
except with the consent of the owner of the patent. Patents are territorial in
effect, e.g. an English patent is only valid in England.*

copyright

*This protects an original work, published or unpublished, which has been
recorded in lasting form. Material protected by copyright include books, plays,
musical compositions, works of art, architectural plans and computer
programmes. The symbol © is used to represent this.*

trademark

*This protects a word, name, symbol, motto or other distinctive form of
identification associated with a product. Examples include Coca–Cola and
McDonalds. The symbol used to represent this is ™.*

how to start a business

So you have a great idea for a business and you've protected it, but now what?

First you have to write a *'business plan'*, which is what every successful
businessperson and entrepreneur does.

There are **four** reasons for a business plan:

 to provide information about your intentions – initially for yourself
and then for others

 to persuade a third party (bank or investors) to provide resources or
assistance, i.e. money

 to help your strategic thinking so you know what you are trying to
achieve and how you are going to achieve it

 to set financial targets so you can forecast your income and
your outgoings

When you are writing a business plan you have to:
- **be realistic**
- **show that you have done your research (don't exaggerate)**
- **understand your business**
- **identify who your customers are, what their needs are and how you are going to tell them about your service**
- **be aware of the competition**

OK, so let's take a closer look at this in reality. Let's look at opening an animal-care facility, for example. I am a banker and you, or your parent, are coming to me (the banker) for a loan. However, someone else has had the same idea and so I am going to interview both of you. Look at the answers to the questions and tell me who you would lend money to.

banker: why open this business?

applicant 1: The timing is right for starting this venture. Animals are playing a larger role in our lives and working people are choosing to provide them with a good life. Loving families with active pets and an active conscience are in search of better lives for their pets and peace of mind for themselves. As a result animal lovers are flocking to an ever-growing number of animal day care facilities across the nation.

applicant 2: Well I have read that this is a growing business and there is easy money to be made from opening up one of them. It is a licence to print money!

banker: what exactly is your mission or goal in setting up this facility?

applicant 1: We want to provide excellent animal care in a pet-friendly atmosphere while ensuring our customers, both pet and owner, receive excellent service in a playful, safe environment.

applicant 2: What exactly do you mean by mission? If you mean make as much money as possible, then, yes, that is our mission.

banker: what do you believe are the keys to your success?

applicant 1: We believe there are 5 reasons to do this and they are as follows:

1. superior customer service – 24-hour high-quality care and service
2. environment – provide a clean, upscale, enjoyable environment conducive to giving a professional trusting service
3. convenience – offer clients a wide range of services in one environment
4. location – an easily accessible location for customer convenience
5. reputation – credibility, integrity and 100 percent dedication

applicant 2: The keys to our success are getting as much business as we can in as fast a time as possible. If we can open up with minding lots of dogs then we are on a winner.

banker: who are your competitors?

applicant 1: The competition comes in several forms. There are several organizations that offer one or two services at their location.

*   There are eight dog care facilities in our area, none of which offer 24-hour day care, making it inconvenient for clients to pick up their pet by a specified time
*   There are 73 grooming and boarding combined facilities and 18 dog training and obedience facilities in our area
*   Our company offers complete and total services at one location. One-stop high-quality pet care for customer convenience

applicant 2: There aren't that many actually. I am not so sure of the numbers but I believe not many at all.

banker: is there a future for this business?

applicant 1: Sharing our lives with our pets provides owners with affection, companionship and security. For busy families, professionals and single pet owners, our company offers them peace of mind as an alternative to leaving their pets home alone.

*   Over 350,000 households in our area have dogs
*   The nation's 58 million pet owners spent an estimated 22.7 billion on their pets last year according to the Pet Industry Joint Advisory Council
*   A survey of pet owners who took their animals to a vet found that nearly a third said they spend more time with their pets than with their friends

Animals are playing a larger role in our lives and working people are choosing to provide them with a good life, which is why we believe this is a growing business.

applicant 2: Definitely. We are buying more and more pets each year and people always need somewhere to put them when they go on holidays, so this business will only get bigger.

banker: what will give your company the edge?

applicant 1: Our company starts with a critical competitive edge: there is no competitor that can claim several multiple services, 24-hour care and customer convenience at one location.

applicant 2: We are well known in the area and we know lots of people with pets. We are also really good with animals.

banker: how are you going to tell everyone about your business?

applicant 1: Our marketing strategy is a simple one – satisfied customers are our best marketing tool. When a customer leaves our business with a happy pet knowing that it has had a fulfilled day, our name and service will stand on its own.

We also plan to host an open house with a business card drawing for one free service. We will offer discounts for the next six months to establish a client base. For example:

- 10 wash your own dog = one free visit gift certificate
- 10 day care visits = one free overnight gift certificate
- create special packages = one day and one night at a special discount price
- multiple pets from the same family = family discount rate
- use promotional items such as Frisbees, collars, coffee mugs, etc. with our logo imprinted

applicant 2: We are going to have flyers dropped into every house in the neighbourhood and we are going to go on local radio to promote our new business – all at the bank will of course be invited!

banker: may i have a copy of your business plan?

Applicant 1: Sure you can. Here it is.

applicant 2: Business plan? Of course you can. I don't have it on me but I will drop it in to you in the next few days.

Now, *which* person would you lend to?

Every entrepreneur should write a business plan, as it gives them direction and focus. If you're planning to set up a business, this will help give others confidence in you if you are looking for their support – especially if it's financial or technical support.

wealth is all around you – or is it?

Each day, you see people who are not as smart as you are making money.

Take a look around you; just about everything you can see right now is the result of a business that someone owns.

Just about everything you use was created by someone, and manufactured, sold, serviced or shipped by someone's business.

So, get thinking about which business you believe would be a success – and you never know, you could be the next Sir Richard Branson, Ben Cohen and Jerry Greenfield or Mark Zuckerberg.

chapter 6
the stock market

A *stock market* is a private or public market that is used for the buying and selling of *shares* in companies that are quoted on a particular stock exchange.

Shares are fractions or units of companies that are sold to people like you and me, so that when you buy a share in a company you actually own a small piece of it.

why do companies sell shares?

Companies sell stock in their businesses in order to generate money that will allow them to grow and expand or maybe even will allow them to fund the buying of other companies.

They might not be able to keep growing on their own so they sell parts of their company to you and me and we then become shareholders in that company. Alternatively, if you set up a business (*see last chapter*) you might issue shares in order to grow.

why do people buy shares?

People do this because they want to make more money. This can happen in one of two ways – *dividends* and *share value increases*, outlined in more detail below:

dividends
This is a sum of money that each shareholder is given when the company makes a profit. The company decides how much they are going to give to shareholders for each share they hold. So, the more shares you hold, the more money in dividends you will receive.

share value increases

This is how most money from investing in shares is made. The price of a share will go up when people want to buy a piece of a company because they feel the company is going to become more successful than it already is. However, if people want to sell their shares and there aren't too many people willing to buy them then the share price will go down.

The trick or secret to becoming successful when buying and selling shares is to 'buy low and sell high.' [This is not as easy as it may sound or we would all make money from the stock market!]

how do you buy shares?

If you want to buy or sell shares you will need the help of a stockbroker – either an individual or a company who is authorized to trade shares on the stock exchange. They are paid a fee or commission for this service. Some stockbrokers will carry out what is called an *execution only* transaction where they carry out your specific orders to buy or sell shares while others offer investment ideas and financial guidance.

types of shares

There are three main recognized types of share – penny stocks, growth stocks and blue-chip stocks. Each is explained in more detail below:

penny stocks

These are shares in very small companies, often ones that are involved in experimental products, new technologies or even new markets. As such they can be subject to rapid growth or equally rapid decline!

People invest in these shares because they are cheap, thinking they are great value. Now as tempting as it might be, as a new investor in the future you should probably stay away from these smaller priced shares to begin with.

growth stocks

These are shares in companies that may be growing rapidly or are seen to have potential for success in the future.

Many of these companies are developing new and innovative products that might be, for example, better and more environmentally friendly than existing products. They might be developing new forms of cleaner energy. Many new technology-based companies are considered growth stocks.

blue-chip stocks

These are shares in well-established companies that have a track record of increasing revenue and producing profits.

They are called *blue chip* because this is the colour of the highest-value chip used in gambling casinos. They offer a reasonably safe investment and are likely to neither fall nor rise dramatically. However, when major changes occur in the national and world economy, as is currently happening, then even blue chip stocks are in danger of collapsing (a prime example of this is the value of banking shares over the past two years – some have lost nearly 90 percent of what they were worth in 2007!). So, never assume they are risk-free either.

ftse 100 index of the top 10 companies

Below is an example of the top 10 companies in the **FTSE100** in terms of their market capitalization as at the end of December 2008:

company	sector	net-market value (£ms)
BP	Oil & Gas Producers	99,112
HSBC Holdings	Banks	79,471
Vodafone Group	Mobile Telecommunications	73,155
GlaxoSmithKline	Pharmaceuticals & Biotechnology	67,313
Royal Dutch Shell A	Oil & Gas Producers	64,030
Royal Dutch Shell B	Oil & Gas Producers	46,893
AstraZeneca	Pharmaceuticals & Biotechnology	40,965
British American Tobacco	Tobacco	35,938
BG Group	Oil & Gas Producers	32,243
BHP Billiton	Mining	28,559
Source: FTSE Group, data as at 31 December 2008.		

it can go down as well as up!

Investing in shares is a *doubled-edged sword* – you can make lots of money if you are successful but equally you could lose it all if you are not!

Remember these two things about shares:

 **never borrow money to buy shares**

only ever invest in them if you can afford to lose all of your money

I know people who borrowed £100,000 to buy shares in a company costing £1 per share because they were told that they would double their money in six months. So they bought shares at £1, which cost them £100,000, and now the shares are worth just 10 pence, meaning that the value of their shares is now £10,000 but they still owe £100,000!

Don't invest in shares in the future unless you can afford to take the lows with the highs!

the 'r' factor

What I am referring to here is the *research factor*. Get on the net!

Before you even think about investing in shares you have to do your homework, which means doing some research before you take the plunge.

You should:

understand how shares operate

get to know the different stock exchanges throughout the world

familiarize yourself with different types of stock and different sectors

look at how companies have performed in the past and how they compare to others in their particular sector

stock-market monopoly

A very good exercise that you and your friends could do easily, which will expose you to the stock market without allowing you to lose any of your well-earned cash, involves practising first.

- pick 3 companies from the FTSE100 and imagine that you are going to invest £1,000 in each of them

- don't just randomly select 3, but do some research on the companies you want a piece of

- you are going to invest £3,000 in total

- give yourself a timeframe of let's say 3 months and then see what the value of your £3,000 has become

- the person who makes the most money wins and gets a prize, say, being treated to lunch, the cinema, a gig

This is really a great way to get used to playing the stock market without actually losing any real money. When the time does come and you want to invest for real you will have some experience and understand what you are getting into.

'bulls' and 'bears'

I am often asked what these terms mean in relation to the stock market:

- **a 'bull' market is the opposite to a 'bear' market and it happens when the share values of companies go up**

- **a 'bear' market is when share values in companies are going down. Just think of the saying a 'bear with a sore head'**

For the past couple of years the world's stockmarkets have been operating in bear markets due to the current world recession. Everyone is hoping that a bull market is not too far away, however, in which share values will rise.

who wants to be a millionaire?

Probably a stupid question. We all do, probably...

In reality, unless you're lucky enough to be born wealthy, the likelihood is unless you win the lottery this might be beyond your reach.

Or is that strictly true? Through hard graft, smart investing and smart thinking, you could potentially be on the road to your millions.

For example, if you are 18 years of age and currently have £1,500 on deposit, if you were to earn or invest £230 every month in a savings plan or in stocks and shares and get a return of 12 percent every year then you will have accumulated **£1 million** by the age of 50!

So it is not impossible to do. If you were able to put aside just £150 per month on top of your £1,500 then you would become a millionaire by the age of 54. The trick or secret though is to make sure you invest your money smartly in areas where the rate of return is much greater than what you would get on deposit in your local bank.

On the other hand, maybe you want to do it before that, maybe you want to be the next Mark Zuckerberg or Ben & Jerry. Hopefully, this book will give you some of the tools to do this and get you thinking whether you want to 'stash or splash'.

conclusion

While you'll never find one book that will cover all there is to know on the subject of dealing with money, *Stash or Splash?* aims to give you the basic tools to enable you to watch and monitor your finances as early as possible.

Money management is something that you will become more experienced at as you get older, but I hope this book has given you some insight and new-found knowledge into this really important subject – information that I know will last you a lifetime and prepare you well for the challenges that you will almost certainly encounter in the future – if you're not dealing with them already.

I strongly believe that apart from health issues, there are few worries worse than dealing with money and that's why it's important to make informed decisions as soon as you can.

Almost every person you know has had to deal with financial difficulties or face tough financial choices during his or her lifetime – and that goes for the extremely rich as well as poor. So, you have to be prepared for the unexpected and the information in this book will give you a sound and very strong foundation from which to start.

Use this book as a guide, a reference, a teaching aid or even as a source of inspiration because if you do that you will already be well on the way to achieving financial security and even success.

– Liam Croke

glossary of terms

account
Record of financial transactions for an asset (usually money) that someone has in their financial institution

account statement
Can be referred to as a loan or savings account statement. This is a record of transactions over a period of time on a person's account. This account does not have to have money in it, it could be an account where you owe money i.e. your annual mortgage account statement

annual percentage rate or apr
The percentage cost of credit charged on a yearly basis. For example, if you borrow £100 for 1 year at 10 percent APR then it will cost you £10 at the end of the year. Every loan has a specific APR so it is key to know the APR when comparing loans offered by different banks

atm card
A debit/cash card that allows customers to withdraw money from an automated teller machine

balance
Amount of money held in a person's account at a particular point in time

bankrupt
A person or company that has been declared to have no money by a court and does not have to pay back any of their debt after their existing assets have been taken away from them

board of directors
Individuals elected by shareholders to oversee and run the management of a corporation like a financial institution

bear market
When the stock market is doing badly and prices are going down

bond
This is a certificate issued by a bank or government for a period of time in order to raise capital by borrowing. A bond is a promise to repay the amount borrowed along with interest on a specified date in the future

budget
Plan or record for saving and spending money

bull market
When the stock market is doing well and prices are going up

consumer
An individual who buys a good for personal use

commission
A fee paid to a stockbroker for buying and selling shares

compound interest
This is when the interest you earn from a bank is added to your savings on a monthly basis and then that interest begins to earn interest also

competition
When other businesses start selling a product or service similar to yours

core investment option
Also called Cash Balance. This is the current balance of the checking account as at the close of business of the previous day

credit
Money given that must be repaid, usually with interest

credit card
A card that allows you to buy things without having to use cash

credit limit
The maximum amount of money you are allowed to spend on a credit card

credit union
A cooperative financial institution that is member owned

currency
Any form of money that is in public circulation

debit card
A card that allows you to withdraw money directly from your savings

debt
Money owed to a person or business

default
The failure to repay a loan

depression
A period marked by high unemployment, when prices for goods drop with no one willing to buy anything with what little money they have

dividend
A payment declared by a company's board of directors and given to its shareholders out of the company's current earnings

economy
When human and natural resources interact to produce goods and services

entrepreneur
Someone who takes a risk in creating a new business and introduces a product they believe will be innovative and something that consumers will want to buy and use

equity release scheme
Equity is the difference between what you owe on a property and what the property is worth, i.e. your property is worth £300,000 and you owe £200,000 then you have 'equity' of £100,000. An Equity release

scheme therefore is where you 'unlock' some of this equity in your home to use for other purposes, i.e. help buy another property, buy land, clear other debts you have like credit cards, car loans etc

foreign exchange market

A place where foreign exchange dealers in cities around the world trade with each other in different currencies

fixed rate

A loan in which the interest rate does not change during the entire term of the loan

ftse uk index series

This is designed to represent the performance of UK companies, providing investors with a comprehensive set of indices that measure the performance of all capital and industry segments of the UK equity market

income

Money earned through employment and investments

income tax

A tax deducted by the government on money earned by workers

inflation

The general price increase of goods and services in an economy

interest

Money you have to pay when you borrow money, or the money a bank pays to you when you have your money on deposit with them

investment

An item of value purchased for income or capital appreciation

investment bank

A financial firm which specializes in the sale and management of securities, such as stocks and bonds, rather than just handling cash funds like a traditional bank.

loan shark

Someone who lends money at excessive rates of interest. Some are often financed and supported by an organized crime network.

market capitalization

A measurement of a corporate or economic size, based on the company's share price multiplied by the number of shares outstanding for a public company. The investment community uses this figure to determine a company's size, as opposed to sales or total asset figures. For example, if a company has 35 million shares outstanding, each with a market value of £100, the company's market capitalization is £3.5 billion (35,000,000 x £100 per share).

market survey

A series of questions asking people what they like and don't like, what services they would use and what they would be willing to pay for them

market value

The value of your securities as of the close of business of the previous day

maturity
Date on which a debt becomes due for payment

mortgage
A loan given by a bank to pay for a house

non standard lender
A lender who makes loans available to people who do not fit the criteria of 'mainstream banks', i.e. they may not be able to prove their income, they may have a poor repayment history etc.

portfolio
A collection of investments all owned by the same individual or company

producer
A person or business that provides goods and services

profit
The money a business makes after deducting its costs in making and selling the good

personal identification number or pin
Your 'secret' number allowing you to use your debit or credit card

recession
When fewer goods are being sold, leading to fewer goods being made, which leads to fewer workers being needed to make them, leading to large-scale unemployment

retirement
The time when you stop working and having a job

savings
Money put into a bank that can be used later for a holiday, college fees or a deposit for a house. It can also used for a 'rainy day', i.e. periods of unemployment when your income reduces

security
An investment or asset offered by an individual or company to a bank that can be taken if they fail to repay a loan

shareholder
A person who owns stock in a company

stock
When you buy part of a company as an investment

stockbroker
A person who buys and sells shares for other people

stock market
A place where shares of stock from different companies can be bought and sold

tax
Money that people and businesses must pay to help support a government

wall street
The home of the New York Stock Exchange

withdrawal
Removal of funds from a place of deposit or investment

acknowledgements

I would like to thank my amazing wife, Roseann.

Not only has she listened to me on a daily basis about this book but her feedback and help has made it what it is.

To say thanks seems so small ... but THANK YOU.

To my children, Rachel, Emily and Sarah, I love you with all my heart.

To all the team in New Holland, thank you so much for sharing my passion and enthusiasm, it was an absolute joy working with you.

index

If you see a page number in **bold**, the term is explained in the glossary.